3 1994 01466 7361

07/12

ID600558

HIP-HOP HEADLINERS

QUEEN LATIFAH

J B LATIFAH KEN
Kennon, Michou
Queen Latifah

$25.25
NEW HOPE   31994014667361

RIGHT ON!

Gareth Stevens
Publishing

By Michou Kennon

Please visit our Web site, www.garethstevens.com. For a free color catalog of all our high-quality books, call toll free 1-800-542-2595 or fax 1-877-542-2596.

Library of Congress Cataloging-in-Publication Data

Kennon, Michou.
 Queen Latifah / Michou Kennon.
    p. cm. — (Hip-hop headliners)
 Includes index.
 ISBN 978-1-4339-4808-4 (library binding)
 ISBN 978-1-4339-4809-1 (pbk.)
 ISBN 978-1-4339-4810-7 (6-pack)
 1. Latifah, Queen—Juvenile literature. 2. Rap musicians—United States—Biography—Juvenile literature. 3. Television actors and actresses—United States—Biography—Juvenile literature. 4. Motion picture actors and actresses—United States—Biography—Juvenile literature. I. Title.
 ML3930.L178K46 2011
 782.421649092—dc22
 [B]
                                    2010029136

First Edition

Published in 2011 by
Gareth Stevens Publishing
111 East 14th Street, Suite 349
New York, NY 10003

Copyright © 2011 Gareth Stevens Publishing

Designer: Haley W. Harasymiw
Editor: Therese Shea

Photo credits: Cover, pp. 2–32 (background) Shutterstock.com; cover (Queen Latifah), p. 1 Andy Lyons/Getty Images; pp. 5, 7, 13, 17, 19 Kevin Winter/Getty Images; p. 9 Mark Mainz/Getty Images; p. 11 Kevin Winter/FOX/ImageDirect; pp. 15, 23 Jon Kopaloff/Getty Images; p. 21 Frank Micelotta/Getty Images for Strategic Group; p. 25 Elsa/Getty Images; p. 27 Alberto E. Rodriguez/Getty Images; p. 29 Frazer Harrison/Getty Images.

Printed in the United States of America

CPSIA compliance information: Batch #CW11GS: For further information contact Gareth Stevens, New York, New York at 1-800-542-2595.

Contents

Queen of Hip-Hop

Queen Latifah was the first woman to become a hip-hop star. She is not just a music star. She is a queen of TV, movies, and business.

Becoming the Queen

Queen Latifah was born on March 18, 1970. She grew up in Newark, New Jersey. Her real name is Dana Owens.

When Dana was 8, a family member called her "Latifah." This name means "sensitive" in Arabic. Dana started to use this name as her own.

Latifah sang in high school shows. She also began rapping in a group called Ladies Fresh. In college, Latifah added "Queen" to her name.

The Queen's Music

In 1989, Queen Latifah released her first album. It was called *All Hail the Queen*. "Ladies First" was a hit song.

13

In 1991, Latifah's second album was not a big hit. Her record company did not want to help her make another album.

In 1992, Latifah's brother died. The next year, Latifah made an album for him. It was called *Black Reign*. It became her biggest hit.

Queen Latifah did more than rap.

She sang R&B. She also made a

jazz album in 2004. She called it

The Dana Owens Album.

Latifah's 2009 album was called *Persona*. It featured Mary J. Blige, Jadakiss, and other hip-hop stars.

Mary J. Blige

21

Acting and More

Queen Latifah has acted in movies and on TV. She starred in the movie *Chicago* in 2002. She won awards for her role.

23

Queen Latifah owns a business that finds new music acts. It also helps others make movies and TV shows.

Latifah wrote a book called *Put on Your Crown*. She shares her life. She tells how she learned to love herself.

Latifah was given a star on the Hollywood Walk of Fame. She was the first hip-hop star to get this award!

EEN LATIFAH

29

Timeline

1970   Dana Owens is born on
March 18 in Newark, New Jersey.

1989   Queen Latifah releases her
first album.

1993   Latifah's *Black Reign* album
becomes her biggest hit.

2002   Latifah sings and acts in the
movie *Chicago*.

2004   *The Dana Owens Album*
comes out.

2006   Latifah gets a star on the
Hollywood Walk of Fame.

2009   Queen Latifah's album *Persona*
is released.

For More Information

Books:

Feinstein, Stephen. *Queen Latifah*. Berkeley Heights, NJ: Enslow Publishers, 2009.

Koestler-Grack, Rachel A. *Queen Latifah*. New York, NY: Chelsea House, 2007.

Snyder, Gail. *Queen Latifah*. Broomall, PA: Mason Crest Publishers, 2007.

Web Sites:

Queen Latifah
www.mtv.com/music/artist/queen_latifah/artist.jhtml

Queen Latifah
www.queenlatifah.com

Glossary

award: a prize given to someone for doing something well

college: a school after high school

R&B: a way to say rhythm and blues. This music has a strong beat and may be sad.

record company: a business that produces and sells music

release: to make ready for use or sale

sensitive: showing care for others' feelings

Index